Connected  Mathematics 2

Data About Us

Statistics

Glenda Lappan
James T. Fey
William M. Fitzgerald
Susan N. Friel
Elizabeth Difanis Phillips

PEARSON

Boston, Massachusetts · Glenview, Illinois · Shoreview, Minnesota · Upper Saddle River, New Jersey

Connected Mathematics™ was developed at Michigan State University with financial support from the Michigan State University Office of the Provost, Computing and Technology, and the College of Natural Science.

This material is based upon work supported by the National Science Foundation under Grant No. MDR 9150217 and Grant No. ESI 9986372. Opinions expressed are those of the authors and not necessarily those of the Foundation.

The Michigan State University authors and administration have agreed that all MSU royalties arising from this publication will be devoted to purposes supported by the MSU Mathematics Education Enrichment Fund.

Acknowledgments appear on page 77, which constitutes an extension of this copyright page.

Authors of Connected Mathematics

(from left to right) Glenda Lappan, Betty Phillips, Susan Friel, Bill Fitzgerald, Jim Fey

Glenda Lappan is a University Distinguished Professor in the Department of Mathematics at Michigan State University. Her research and development interests are in the connected areas of students' learning of mathematics and mathematics teachers' professional growth and change related to the development and enactment of K–12 curriculum materials.

James T. Fey is a Professor of Curriculum and Instruction and Mathematics at the University of Maryland. His consistent professional interest has been development and research focused on curriculum materials that engage middle and high school students in problem-based collaborative investigations of mathematical ideas and their applications.

William M. Fitzgerald (*Deceased*) was a Professor in the Department of Mathematics at Michigan State University. His early research was on the use of concrete materials in supporting student learning and led to the development of teaching materials for laboratory environments. Later he helped develop a teaching model to support student experimentation with mathematics.

Susan N. Friel is a Professor of Mathematics Education in the School of Education at the University of North Carolina at Chapel Hill. Her research interests focus on statistics education for middle-grade students and, more broadly, on teachers' professional development and growth in teaching mathematics K–8.

Elizabeth Difanis Phillips is a Senior Academic Specialist in the Mathematics Department of Michigan State University. She is interested in teaching and learning mathematics for both teachers and students. These interests have led to curriculum and professional development projects at the middle school and high school levels, as well as projects related to the teaching and learning of algebra across the grades.

CMP2 Development Staff

Teacher Collaborator in Residence
Yvonne Grant
Michigan State University

Administrative Assistant
Judith Martus Miller
Michigan State University

Production and Field Site Manager
Lisa Keller
Michigan State University

Technical and Editorial Support
**Brin Keller, Peter Lappan, Jim Laser,
Michael Masterson, Stacey Miceli**

Assessment Team
June Bailey and **Debra Sobko** (Apollo Middle School, Rochester, New York), **George Bright** (University of North Carolina, Greensboro), **Gwen Ranzau Campbell** (Sunrise Park Middle School, White Bear Lake, Minnesota), **Holly DeRosia, Kathy Dole,** and **Teri Keusch** (Portland Middle School, Portland, Michigan), **Mary Beth Schmitt** (Traverse City East Junior High School, Traverse City, Michigan), **Genni Steele** (Central Middle School, White Bear Lake, Minnesota), **Jacqueline Stewart** (Okemos, Michigan), **Elizabeth Tye** (Magnolia Junior High School, Magnolia, Arkansas)

Development Assistants
At Lansing Community College *Undergraduate Assistant:* **James Brinegar**

At Michigan State University *Graduate Assistants:* **Dawn Berk, Emily Bouck, Bulent Buyukbozkirli, Kuo-Liang Chang, Christopher Danielson, Srinivasa Dharmavaram, Deb Johanning, Kelly Rivette, Sarah Sword, Tat Ming Sze, Marie Turini, Jeffrey Wanko;** *Undergraduate Assistants:* **Daniel Briggs, Jeffrey Chapin, Jade Corsé, Elisha Hardy, Alisha Harold, Elizabeth Keusch, Julia Letoutchaia, Karen Loeffler, Brian Oliver, Carl Oliver, Evonne Pedawi, Lauren Rebrovich**

At the University of Maryland *Graduate Assistants:* **Kim Harris Bethea, Kara Karch**

At the University of North Carolina (Chapel Hill) *Graduate Assistants:* **Mark Ellis, Trista Stearns;** *Undergraduate Assistant:* **Daniel Smith**

Advisory Board for CMP2

Thomas Banchoff
Professor of Mathematics
Brown University
Providence, Rhode Island

Anne Bartel
Mathematics Coordinator
Minneapolis Public Schools
Minneapolis, Minnesota

Hyman Bass
Professor of Mathematics
University of Michigan
Ann Arbor, Michigan

Joan Ferrini-Mundy
Associate Dean of the College of
Natural Science; Professor
Michigan State University
East Lansing, Michigan

James Hiebert
Professor
University of Delaware
Newark, Delaware

Susan Hudson Hull
Charles A. Dana Center
University of Texas
Austin, Texas

Michele Luke
Mathematics Curriculum
Coordinator
West Junior High
Minnetonka, Minnesota

Kay McClain
Assistant Professor of
Mathematics Education
Vanderbilt University
Nashville, Tennessee

Edward Silver
Professor; Chair of Educational
Studies
University of Michigan
Ann Arbor, Michigan

Judith Sowder
Professor Emerita
San Diego State University
San Diego, California

Lisa Usher
Mathematics Resource Teacher
California Academy of
Mathematics and Science
San Pedro, California

Field Test Sites for CMP2

During the development of the revised edition of *Connected Mathematics* (CMP2), more than 100 classroom teachers have field-tested materials at 49 school sites in 12 states and the District of Columbia. This classroom testing occurred over three academic years (2001 through 2004), allowing careful study of the effectiveness of each of the 24 units that comprise the program. A special thanks to the students and teachers at these pilot schools.

Arkansas

Magnolia Public Schools
Kittena Bell*, Judith Trowell*; *Central Elementary School:* Maxine Broom, Betty Eddy, Tiffany Fallin, Bonnie Flurry, Carolyn Monk, Elizabeth Tye; *Magnolia Junior High School:* Monique Bryan, Ginger Cook, David Graham, Shelby Lamkin

Colorado

Boulder Public Schools
Nevin Platt Middle School: Judith Koenig

St. Vrain Valley School District, Longmont
Westview Middle School: Colleen Beyer, Kitty Canupp, Ellie Decker*, Peggy McCarthy, Tanya deNobrega, Cindy Payne, Ericka Pilon, Andrew Roberts

District of Columbia

Capitol Hill Day School: Ann Lawrence

Georgia

University of Georgia, Athens
Brad Findell

Madison Public Schools
Morgan County Middle School: Renee Burgdorf, Lynn Harris, Nancy Kurtz, Carolyn Stewart

Maine

Falmouth Public Schools
Falmouth Middle School: Donna Erikson, Joyce Hebert, Paula Hodgkins, Rick Hogan, David Legere, Cynthia Martin, Barbara Stiles, Shawn Towle*

Michigan

Portland Public Schools
Portland Middle School: Mark Braun, Holly DeRosia, Kathy Dole*, Angie Foote, Teri Keusch, Tammi Wardwell

Traverse City Area Public Schools
Bertha Vos Elementary: Kristin Sak; *Central Grade School:* Michelle Clark; Jody Meyers; *Eastern Elementary:* Karrie Tufts; *Interlochen Elementary:* Mary McGee-Cullen; *Long Lake Elementary:* Julie Faulkner*, Charlie Maxbauer, Katherine Sleder; *Norris Elementary:* Hope Slanaker; *Oak Park Elementary:* Jessica Steed; *Traverse Heights Elementary:* Jennifer Wolfert; *Westwoods Elementary:* Nancy Conn; *Old Mission Peninsula School:* Deb Larimer; *Traverse City East Junior High:* Ivanka Berkshire, Ruthanne Kladder, Jan Palkowski, Jane Peterson, Mary Beth Schmitt; *Traverse City West Junior High:* Dan Fouch*, Ray Fouch

Sturgis Public Schools
Sturgis Middle School: Ellen Eisele

Minnesota

Burnsville School District 191
Hidden Valley Elementary: Stephanie Cin, Jane McDevitt

Hopkins School District 270
Alice Smith Elementary: Sandra Cowing, Kathleen Gustafson, Martha Mason, Scott Stillman; *Eisenhower Elementary:* Chad Bellig, Patrick Berger, Nancy Glades, Kye Johnson, Shane Wasserman, Victoria Wilson; *Gatewood Elementary:* Sarah Ham, Julie Kloos, Janine Pung, Larry Wade; *Glen Lake Elementary:* Jacqueline Cramer, Kathy Hering, Cecelia Morris,

Robb Trenda; *Katherine Curren Elementary:* Diane Bancroft, Sue DeWit, John Wilson; *L. H. Tanglen Elementary:* Kevin Athmann, Lisa Becker, Mary LaBelle, Kathy Rezac, Roberta Severson; *Meadowbrook Elementary:* Jan Gauger, Hildy Shank, Jessica Zimmerman; *North Junior High:* Laurel Hahn, Kristin Lee, Jodi Markuson, Bruce Mestemacher, Laurel Miller, Bonnie Rinker, Jeannine Salzer, Sarah Shafer, Cam Stottler; *West Junior High:* Alicia Beebe, Kristie Earl, Nobu Fujii, Pam Georgetti, Susan Gilbert, Regina Nelson Johnson, Debra Lindstrom, Michele Luke*, Jon Sorenson

Minneapolis School District 1
Ann Sullivan K-8 School: Bronwyn Collins; Anne Bartel* (Curriculum and Instruction Office)

Wayzata School District 284
Central Middle School: Sarajane Myers, Dan Nielsen, Tanya Ravenholdt

White Bear Lake School District 624
Central Middle School: Amy Jorgenson, Michelle Reich, Brenda Sammon

New York

New York City Public Schools
IS 89: Yelena Aynbinder, Chi-Man Ng, Nina Rapaport, Joel Spengler, Phyllis Tam*, Brent Wyso; *Wagner Middle School:* Jason Appel, Intissar Fernandez, Yee Gee Get, Richard Goldstein, Irving Marcus, Sue Norton, Bernadita Owens, Jennifer Rehn*, Kevin Yuhas

---

* indicates a Field Test Site Coordinator

Ohio

Talawanda School District, Oxford
Talawanda Middle School: Teresa Abrams, Larry Brock, Heather Brosey, Julie Churchman, Monna Even, Karen Fitch, Bob George, Amanda Klee, Pat Meade, Sandy Montgomery, Barbara Sherman, Lauren Steidl

Miami University
Jeffrey Wanko*

Springfield Public Schools
Rockway School: Jim Mamer

Pennsylvania

Pittsburgh Public Schools
Kenneth Labuskes, Marianne O'Connor, Mary Lynn Raith*; *Arthur J. Rooney Middle School:* David Hairston, Stamatina Mousetis, Alfredo Zangaro; *Frick International Studies Academy:* Suzanne Berry, Janet Falkowski, Constance Finseth, Romika Hodge, Frank Machi; *Reizenstein Middle School:* Jeff Baldwin, James Brautigam, Lorena Burnett, Glen Cobbett, Michael Jordan, Margaret Lazur, Melissa Munnell, Holly Neely, Ingrid Reed, Dennis Reft

Texas

Austin Independent School District
Bedichek Middle School: Lisa Brown, Jennifer Glasscock, Vicki Massey

El Paso Independent School District
Cordova Middle School: Armando Aguirre, Anneliesa Durkes, Sylvia Guzman, Pat Holguin*, William Holguin, Nancy Nava, Laura Orozco, Michelle Peña, Roberta Rosen, Patsy Smith, Jeremy Wolf

Plano Independent School District
Patt Henry, James Wohlgehagen*; *Frankford Middle School:* Mandy Baker, Cheryl Butsch, Amy Dudley, Betsy Eshelman, Janet Greene, Cort Haynes, Kathy Letchworth, Kay Marshall, Kelly McCants, Amy Reck, Judy Scott, Syndy Snyder, Lisa Wang; *Wilson Middle School:* Darcie Bane, Amanda Bedenko, Whitney Evans, Tonelli Hatley, Sarah (Becky) Higgs, Kelly Johnston, Rebecca McElligott, Kay Neuse, Cheri Slocum, Kelli Straight

Washington

Evergreen School District
Shahala Middle School: Nicole Abrahamsen, Terry Coon*, Carey Doyle, Sheryl Drechsler, George Gemma, Gina Helland, Amy Hilario, Darla Lidyard, Sean McCarthy, Tilly Meyer, Willow Neuwelt, Todd Parsons, Brian Pederson, Stan Posey, Shawn Scott, Craig Sjoberg, Lynette Sundstrom, Charles Switzer, Luke Youngblood

Wisconsin

Beaver Dam Unified School District
Beaver Dam Middle School: Jim Braemer, Jeanne Frick, Jessica Greatens, Barbara Link, Dennis McCormick, Karen Michels, Nancy Nichols*, Nancy Palm, Shelly Stelsel, Susan Wiggins

---

* indicates a Field Test Site Coordinator

Reviews of CMP to Guide Development of CMP2

Before writing for CMP2 began or field tests were conducted, the first edition of *Connected Mathematics* was submitted to the mathematics faculties of school districts from many parts of the country and to 80 individual reviewers for extensive comments.

School District Survey Reviews of CMP

Arizona
Madison School District #38 (Phoenix)

Arkansas
Cabot School District, Little Rock School District, Magnolia School District

California
Los Angeles Unified School District

Colorado
St. Vrain Valley School District (Longmont)

Florida
Leon County Schools (Tallahassee)

Illinois
School District #21 (Wheeling)

Indiana
Joseph L. Block Junior High (East Chicago)

Kentucky
Fayette County Public Schools (Lexington)

Maine
Selection of Schools

Massachusetts
Selection of Schools

Michigan
Sparta Area Schools

Minnesota
Hopkins School District

Texas
Austin Independent School District, The El Paso Collaborative for Academic Excellence, Plano Independent School District

Wisconsin
Platteville Middle School

Individual Reviewers of CMP

Arkansas
Deborah Cramer; Robby Frizzell *(Taylor)*; Lowell Lynde *(University of Arkansas, Monticello)*; Leigh Manzer *(Norfork)*; Lynne Roberts *(Emerson High School, Emerson)*; Tony Timms *(Cabot Public Schools)*; Judith Trowell *(Arkansas Department of Higher Education)*

California
José Alcantar *(Gilroy)*; Eugenie Belcher *(Gilroy)*; Marian Pasternack *(Lowman M. S. T. Center, North Hollywood)*; Susana Pezoa *(San Jose)*; Todd Rabusin *(Hollister)*; Margaret Siegfried *(Ocala Middle School, San Jose)*; Polly Underwood *(Ocala Middle School, San Jose)*

Colorado
Janeane Golliher *(St. Vrain Valley School District, Longmont)*; Judith Koenig *(Nevin Platt Middle School, Boulder)*

Florida
Paige Loggins *(Swift Creek Middle School, Tallahassee)*

Illinois
Jan Robinson *(School District #21, Wheeling)*

Indiana
Frances Jackson *(Joseph L. Block Junior High, East Chicago)*

Kentucky
Natalee Feese *(Fayette County Public Schools, Lexington)*

Maine
Betsy Berry *(Maine Math & Science Alliance, Augusta)*

Maryland
Joseph Gagnon *(University of Maryland, College Park)*; Paula Maccini *(University of Maryland, College Park)*

Massachusetts
George Cobb *(Mt. Holyoke College, South Hadley)*; Cliff Kanold *(University of Massachusetts, Amherst)*

Michigan
Mary Bouck *(Farwell Area Schools)*; Carol Dorer *(Slauson Middle School, Ann Arbor)*; Carrie Heaney *(Forsythe Middle School, Ann Arbor)*; Ellen Hopkins *(Clague Middle School, Ann Arbor)*; Teri Keusch *(Portland Middle School, Portland)*; Valerie Mills *(Oakland Schools, Waterford)*; Mary Beth Schmitt *(Traverse City East Junior High, Traverse City)*; Jack Smith *(Michigan State University, East Lansing)*; Rebecca Spencer *(Sparta Middle School, Sparta)*; Ann Marie Nicoll Turner *(Tappan Middle School, Ann Arbor)*; Scott Turner *(Scarlett Middle School, Ann Arbor)*

Minnesota
Margarita Alvarez *(Olson Middle School, Minneapolis)*; Jane Amundson *(Nicollet Junior High, Burnsville)*; Anne Bartel *(Minneapolis Public Schools)*; Gwen Ranzau Campbell *(Sunrise Park Middle School, White Bear Lake)*; Stephanie Cin *(Hidden Valley Elementary, Burnsville)*; Joan Garfield *(University of Minnesota, Minneapolis)*; Gretchen Hall *(Richfield Middle School, Richfield)*; Jennifer Larson *(Olson Middle School, Minneapolis)*; Michele Luke *(West Junior High, Minnetonka)*; Jeni Meyer *(Richfield Junior High, Richfield)*; Judy Pfingsten *(Inver Grove Heights Middle School, Inver Grove Heights)*; Sarah Shafer *(North Junior High, Minnetonka)*; Genni Steele *(Central Middle School, White Bear Lake)*; Victoria Wilson *(Eisenhower Elementary, Hopkins)*; Paul Zorn *(St. Olaf College, Northfield)*

New York
Debra Altenau-Bartolino *(Greenwich Village Middle School, New York)*; Doug Clements *(University of Buffalo)*; Francis Curcio *(New York University, New York)*; Christine Dorosh *(Clinton School for Writers, Brooklyn)*; Jennifer Rehn *(East Side Middle School, New York)*; Phyllis Tam *(IS 89 Lab School, New York)*;

Marie Turini *(Louis Armstrong Middle School, New York)*; Lucy West *(Community School District 2, New York)*; Monica Witt *(Simon Baruch Intermediate School 104, New York)*

Pennsylvania
Robert Aglietti *(Pittsburgh)*; Sharon Mihalich *(Pittsburgh)*; Jennifer Plumb *(South Hills Middle School, Pittsburgh)*; Mary Lynn Raith *(Pittsburgh Public Schools)*

Texas
Michelle Bittick *(Austin Independent School District)*; Margaret Cregg *(Plano Independent School District)*; Sheila Cunningham *(Klein Independent School District)*; Judy Hill *(Austin Independent School District)*; Patricia Holguin *(El Paso Independent School District)*; Bonnie McNemar *(Arlington)*; Kay Neuse *(Plano Independent School District)*; Joyce Polanco *(Austin Independent School District)*; Marge Ramirez *(University of Texas at El Paso)*; Pat Rossman *(Baker Campus, Austin)*; Cindy Schimek *(Houston)*; Cynthia Schneider *(Charles A. Dana Center, University of Texas at Austin)*; Uri Treisman *(Charles A. Dana Center, University of Texas at Austin)*; Jacqueline Weilmuenster *(Grapevine-Colleyville Independent School District)*; LuAnn Weynand *(San Antonio)*; Carmen Whitman *(Austin Independent School District)*; James Wohlgehagen *(Plano Independent School District)*

Washington
Ramesh Gangolli *(University of Washington, Seattle)*

Wisconsin
Susan Lamon *(Marquette University, Hales Corner)*; Steve Reinhart *(retired, Chippewa Falls Middle School, Eau Claire)*

Table of Contents

Data About Us
Statistics

Data About Us

What is the greatest number of pets owned by students in your class? How can you find out?

Suppose two classes competed in a jump-rope contest. They recorded the number of jumps for each student. How would you determine which class did better?

A group of students collected data on the number of movies they watched last month. How would you find out the "typical" number of movies watched?

Every 10 years the United States government conducts a *census*, or survey, of every household in the country. The census gathers information about many things including education, employment, and income. Because people are naturally curious about themselves and others, many people are interested in information from the census. Of course, collecting data from every household in the United States is a huge task.

You often hear people making statements about the results of surveys. For example, what does it mean when reports say the average middle-school student has four people in his or her family, or watches three hours of television on a weekday?

In *Data About Us,* you will learn to collect and analyze data for situations similar to those on the previous page. You will also learn to use your results to describe people and their characteristics.

Mathematical Highlights

Statistics

In *Data About Us*, you will explore ways of collecting, organizing, displaying, and analyzing data.

You will learn how to

- Conduct data investigations by posing questions, collecting and analyzing data, and making interpretations to answer questions
- Represent distributions of data using line plots, bar graphs, stem-and-leaf plots, and coordinate graphs
- Compute the mean, median, mode, or range of the data
- Distinguish between categorical data and numerical data and identify which graphs and statistics may be used to represent each kind of data
- Choose the most appropriate statistical measures (mean, median, mode, range, etc.) to describe a distribution of data
- Develop strategies for comparing distributions of data

As you work on problems in this unit, ask yourself questions about situations that involve data analysis:

What is the question being asked?

What organization of the data can help me analyze the data?

What statistical measures will provide useful information about the distribution of data?

What will statistical measures tell me about the distribution of the data?

How can I use graphs and statistics to describe a data distribution or to compare two data distributions in order to answer my original question?

Unit Project

Is Anyone Typical?

What are the characteristics of a typical middle-school student? Who is interested in knowing these characteristics? Does a typical middle-school student really exist? As you proceed through this unit, you will identify some "typical" facts about your classmates, such as these:

- The typical number of letters in a student's full name
- The typical number of people in a student's household
- The typical height of a student

When you have completed the investigations in *Data About Us,* you will carry out a statistical investigation to answer this question:

What are some of the characteristics of a typical middle-school student?

These characteristics may include

- Physical characteristics (for example, age, height, or eye color)
- Family and home characteristics (for example, number of brothers and sisters or number of MP3 players)
- Behaviors (for example, hobbies or number of hours spent watching television)
- Preferences, opinions, or attitudes (for example, favorite musical group, or choice for class president)

As you study this unit, make and improve your plans for your project. Keep in mind that a statistical investigation involves posing questions, collecting data, analyzing data, and interpreting the results of the analysis. As you work through each investigation, think about how you might use what you are learning to help you with your project.

Looking at Data

The problems in this investigation involve people's names. Family traditions are often involved when a child is named. A person's name may reveal information about his or her ancestors.

Many people have interesting stories about how they were named. Here is one student's story: "I'm a twin, and my mom and dad didn't know they were going to have twins. My sister was born first. She was named Sukey. I was a surprise. My mom named me after the woman in the next hospital bed. Her name was Takara."

- Do you know anything interesting about how you were named or about the history behind your family's name?

Rhoshandiatellyneshiaunneveshenk Koyaanisquatsiuth Williams is the longest name on a birth certificate.

Shortly after Rhoshandiatellyneshiaunneveshenk was born, her father lengthened her first name to 1,019 letters and her middle name to 36 letters. What is a good nickname for her?

1.1 Organizing and Interpreting Data

Most parents do not worry about the number of letters in their children's names. Sometimes though, name length does matter. For example, only a limited number of letters may fit on a bracelet or a library card.

Getting Ready for Problem 1.1

What do you think is the typical number of letters in the full names (first and last names) of your classmates?

- What data do you need to collect and how would you collect it?
- How would you organize and represent your data?
- If a new student joined your class today, how might you use your results to predict the length of that student's name?

The students in Ms. Jee's class made a **line plot** to display the distribution of their class's data.

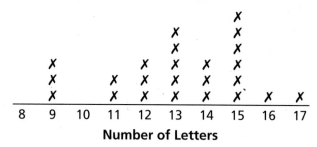

Name Lengths of Ms. Jee's Students

Another group displayed the same data using a **bar graph.**

Name Lengths of Ms. Jee's Students

To describe how the data are distributed, you might look at where the data values cluster, how much they vary, and the high and low values.

Problem 1.1 Organizing and Interpreting Data

Examine the line plot and the bar graph.

A. Describe the distribution of the data. Do you see any patterns?

B. How are the two graphs alike? How are they different?

C. How can you use each graph to determine the total number of letters in all the names?

D. Fahimeh Ghomizadeh said, "My name has the most letters, but the bar that shows my name length is one of the shortest on the graph. Why?" How would you answer this question?

E. Collect the data for your class's name lengths. Represent the data distribution using a line plot or a bar graph.

F. What are some similarities and differences between the data distribution from Ms. Jee's class and the data distribution from your class?

ACE Homework starts on page 21.

Did You Know?

In Africa, a child's name is often very meaningful. Names such as Sekelaga, which means "rejoice," and Tusajigwe, which means "we are blessed," reflect the happiness the family felt at the child's birth. Names such as Mvula, meaning "rain," reflect events that happened at the time the child was born.

Go Online
PHSchool.com

For: Information about African names
Web Code: ame-9031

1.2 Useful Statistics

In the data for Ms. Jee's class, the name length of 15 letters occurs most often. Notice that 15 has the highest stack of X's in the line plot and the tallest bar in the bar graph. We call the most frequent value the **mode** of the data set.

The least value and the greatest value are important values in a data set. They give a sense of the variability in the data. In Ms. Jee's class, the data vary from 9 letters to 17 letters. The difference between the least value and the greatest value is called the **range** of the data. The range of Ms. Jee's class data is 17–9, or 8 letters.

Still another important statistic is the **median,** or the midpoint, of the data set.

The table and line plot below show the distribution of the name-length data for Mr. Gray's class. Notice that these data have two modes, 11 letters and 12 letters. We say the distribution is *bimodal*. The data vary from 7 letters to 19 letters. The range of the data is 19 − 7, or 12 letters.

Name Lengths of Mr. Gray's Students	
Name	**Number of Letters**
Jeffrey Piersonjones	19
Thomas Petes	11
Clarence Jenkins	15
Michelle Hughes	14
Shoshana White	13
Deborah Black	12
Terry Van Bourgondien	19
Maxi Swanson	11
Tonya Stewart	12
Jorge Bastante	13
Richard Mudd	11
Joachim Caruso	13
Robert Northcott	15
Tony Tung	8
Joshua Klein	11
Jan Wong	7
Bob King	7
Veronica Rodriguez	17
Charlene Greene	14
Peter Juliano	12
Linora Haynes	12

Name Lengths of Mr. Gray's Students

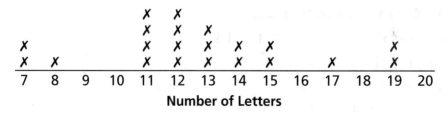

Here is a way to help you think about how to identify the median. Cut a strip of 21 squares from a sheet of grid paper. Each square is for the length of a student's name in Mr. Gray's class. Write the name lengths of Mr. Gray's students in order from least to greatest on the grid paper as shown.

7	7	8	11	11	11	11	12	12	12	12	13	13	13	14	14	15	15	17	19	19

A. Fold the strip in half.

　1. On what number is the crease caused by the fold?

　2. How many numbers occur to the left of this number?

　3. How many numbers occur to the right of this number?

　4. The median is the value of the midpoint marker in a set of data. The same number of data values occur before and after this value. What is the median for these data?

B. Suppose a new student, Suzanne Mannerstrale, joins Mr. Gray's class. The class now has 22 students. On a strip of 22 squares, list the name lengths, including Suzanne's, in order from least to greatest. Fold the strip in half.

　1. On what number is the crease caused by the fold?

　2. How many numbers occur to the left of the crease?

　3. How many numbers occur to the right of the crease?

　4. What is the median for these data?

C. Suzanne has six pets. She made the line plot shown of her pets' name lengths. Find the median length of her pets' names. Find the mode for the data set.

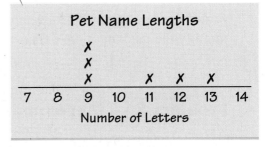

D. There are 15 students in a class. Use the information about the class's name lengths below.

- Mode: 12 letters

- Median: 12 letters

- The data vary from 8 letters to 16 letters

　1. Find a possible set of name lengths for the class.

　2. Make a line plot to display your data distribution.

　3. Compare your graph with the graphs of your classmates. How are the graphs alike? How are they different?

ACE **Homework starts on page 21.**

You can use the median and the mode of a set of data to describe what is typical about the distribution. They are sometimes called *measures of center*.

Use the following ten names. Write each name on an index card. On the back of each card, write the number of letters in the name. A sample index card is shown below.

Student Name Lengths

Name	Number of Letters
Thomas Petes	11
Michelle Hughes	14
Shoshana White	13
Deborah Black	12
Tonya Stewart	12
Richard Mudd	11
Tony Tung	8
Janice Wong	10
Bobby King	9
Charlene Greene	14

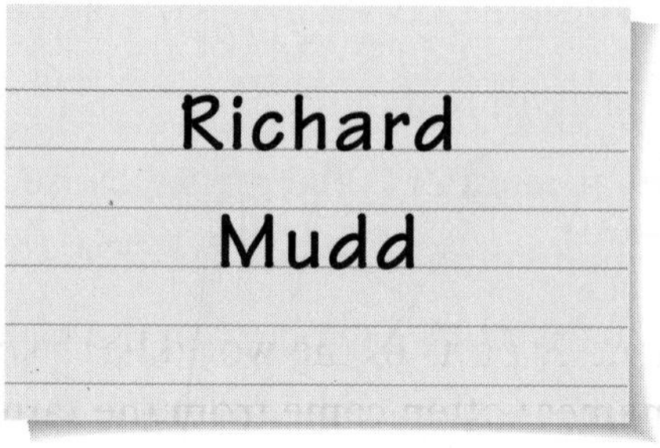

Richard Mudd

front

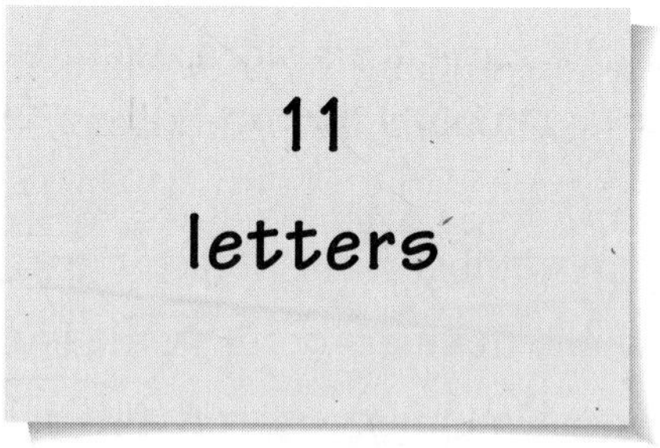

11 letters

back

Order the cards from shortest name length to longest name length, and identify the median of the data.

Problem 1.3 Experimenting With the Median

Use your cards to complete each task below. Keep a record of your work.

A. Remove two names from the original data set so that

   1. the median stays the same.

   2. the median increases.

   3. the median decreases.

B. Add two new names to the original data set so that

    1. the median stays the same.

    2. the median increases.

    3. the median decreases.

C. How does the median of the original data set change if you add a name

    1. with 16 letters?

    2. with 1,019 letters?

ACE Homework starts on page 21.

Did You Know?

Names from many parts of the world have special origins. European family names (last names) often came from the father's first name. For example, Ian Robertson was the son of Robert, Janos Ivanovich was the son (vich) of Ivan, and John Peters was the son of Peter.

Family names also came from words that described a person's hometown or job. This resulted in such names as William Hill and Gilbert Baker.

Family names in China and Vietnam are almost always one-syllable words that are related to names of ruling families. Chang is one such example.

You can read more about names in books such as *Names from Africa* by Ogonna Chuks-Orji and *Do People Grow on Family Trees?* by Ira Wolfman.

Go Online
PHSchool.com **For:** Information about names
Web Code: ame-9031

Using Different Data Types

When you are interested in learning more about something, you ask questions about it. Some questions have answers that are words or categories. For example, what is your favorite sport? Other questions have answers that are numbers. For example, how many inches tall are you?

Categorical data are data that have been grouped into categories, such as "favorite sport." They are usually not numbers. Suppose you ask people in which month they were born or what kinds of pets they have. Their answers would be categorical data.

Numerical data are data that are counts or measures. Suppose you ask people how tall they are or how many pets they have. Their responses would be numerical data.

Getting Ready for Problem

Read each of the questions below. Which questions have words or categories as answers? Which questions have numbers as answers?

- In which month were you born?
- What is your favorite kind of pet?
- How many pets do you have?
- Who is your favorite author?
- How much time do you spend watching television in a day?
- What's your highest score in the game?
- How many movies have you watched in the past week?

The kinds of pets people have often depend on where they live. People who live in cities often have small pets. People who live on farms often have large pets. People who live in apartments sometimes cannot have pets at all.

One middle-school class gathered data about their pets by tallying students' responses to these questions:

- What is your favorite kind of pet?
- How many pets do you have?

The students made tables to show the tallies or frequencies. Then they made bar graphs to display the data distributions.

Do you think the students surveyed live in a city, the suburbs, or the country? Explain.

Number of Pets

Number	Frequency
0	2
1	2
2	5
3	4
4	1
5	2
6	3
7	0
8	1
9	1
10	0
11	0
12	1
13	0
14	1
15	0
16	0
17	1
18	0
19	1
20	0
21	1

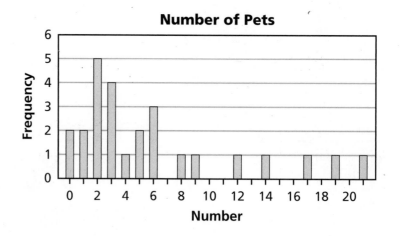

Favorite Kinds of Pets

Pet	Frequency
cat	4
dog	7
fish	2
bird	2
horse	3
goat	1
cow	2
rabbit	3
duck	1
pig	1

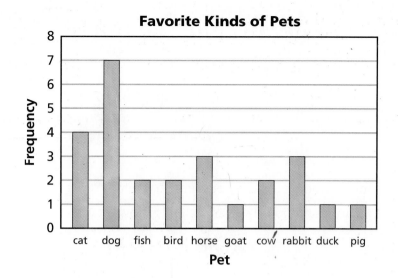

Favorite Kinds of Pets

Problem 1.4 Using Different Data Types

Decide whether each question can be answered by using data from the graphs and tables the students created. If so, give the answer and explain how you got it. If not, explain why not and tell what additional information you would need to answer the question.

A. Which graph shows categorical data?

B. Which graph shows numerical data?

C. What is the total number of pets the students have?

D. What is the greatest number of pets a student has?

E. How many students are in the class?

F. How many students chose cats as their favorite kind of pet?

G. How many cats do students have as pets?

H. What is the mode for the favorite kind of pet?

I. What is the median number of pets students have?

J. What is the range of the numbers of pets students have?

K. Tomas is a student in this class. How many pets does he have?

L. Do the girls have more pets than the boys?

ACE **Homework starts on page 21.**

You have used bar graphs to display distributions of data. *Vertical bar graphs* display data on the horizontal axis with vertical bars. On vertical bar graphs, the heights can be compared to the vertical frequency axis.

Look at the vertical bar graph below.

- What information does the horizontal axis show?
- What information does the vertical axis show?

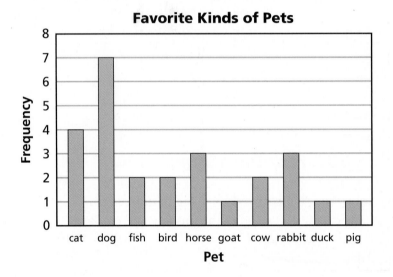

Favorite Kinds of Pets

- How do you find out how many people chose "dog" as their favorite kind of pet using the vertical bar graph?

Suppose five more students are surveyed. Three identify birds as their favorite kind of pet. Two identify cats as their favorite kind of pet.

- What changes would you make in the vertical bar graph to show the new distribution?

Below is the distribution of the original pet data shown on a *horizontal bar graph*.

- Compare the vertical bar graph to the horizontal bar graph. How are they alike? How are they different?

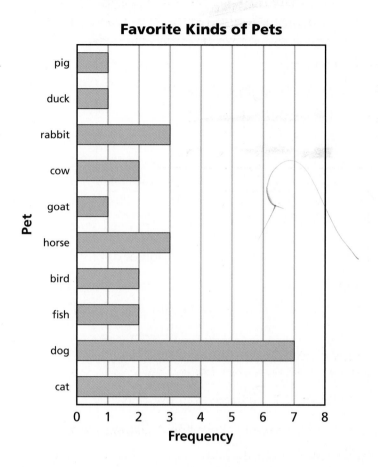

Favorite Kinds of Pets

- How do you find out how many people chose "dog" as their favorite kind of pet using the horizontal bar graph?

Suppose five more students were surveyed. Three identify birds as their favorite kind of pet. Two identify cats as their favorite kind of pet.

- What changes would you make in the horizontal bar graph to show the new distribution?

Below is a vertical bar graph showing the distribution of the number of pets students have.

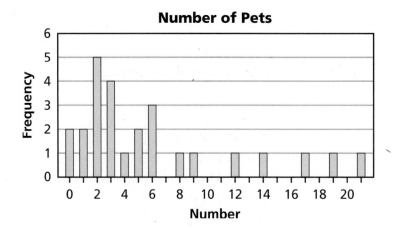

Number of Pets

A. Make a horizontal bar graph to show this distribution of data.

For each question below, explain:

- how you can find the answer to the question using the vertical bar graph
- how you can find the answer to the question using the horizontal bar graph

B. How many students in the class have more than five pets?

C. What is the least number of pets that any student in the class has?

D. What is the greatest number of pets that any student in the class has?

E. What is the median number of pets?

F. Three students were absent when these data were collected. Malcolm has 7 pets, Makana has 1 pet, and Jake has 3 pets. Add their data to each graph. What is the median number of pets now?

ACE Homework starts on page 21.

Applications

For Exercises 1 and 2, use the names of Mr. Young's students listed below.

Ben Foster	Rosita Ramirez
Ava Baker	Kimberly Pace
Lucas Fuentes	Paula Wheeler
Juan Norinda	Darnell Fay
Ron Weaver	Jeremy Yosho
Bryan Wong	Cora Harris
Toby Vanhook	Corey Brooks
Katrina Roberson	Tijuana Degraffenreid

1. Make a table showing the length of each name. Then make both a line plot and a bar graph of the name lengths.

2. What is the typical name length for Mr. Young's students? Use the mode, median, and range to help you answer this question.

For Exercises 3–6, make a line plot or bar graph of a data distribution that fits each description.

3. 24 names, with a range of 12 letters

4. 7 names, with a median length of 14 letters

5. 13 names, with a median length of 13 letters, and with data that vary from 8 letters to 17 letters

6. 16 names, with a median length of $14\frac{1}{2}$ letters, and with data that vary from 11 letters to 20 letters

For Exercises 7–12, use the bar graph below.

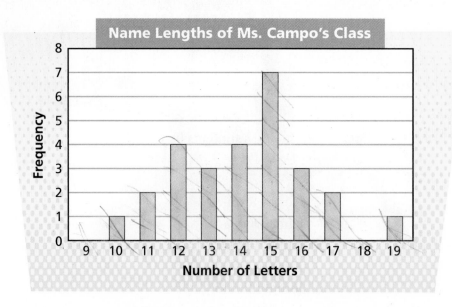

Name Lengths of Ms. Campo's Class

7. How does the data distribution from Ms. Campo's class compare with the data distribution from Mr. Young's class in Exercise 1?

8. **Multiple Choice** For Ms. Campo's students, which value (name length) occurs most frequently?

   A. 12 letters   **B.** 14 letters   **C.** 15 letters   **D.** 16 letters

9. **Multiple Choice** What is the name of the value found in Exercise 8?

   F. range   **G.** median   **H.** mode   **J.** none of these

10. How many students are in Ms. Campo's class? Explain how you got your answer.

11. What is the range of name lengths for this class?

12. What is the median name length? Explain how you got your answer.

13. Look at the table and graph for Number of Pets from the introduction to Problem 1.4. Four new students join the class. One student has 3 pets, two students each have 7 pets, and the last student has 16 pets.

   a. Copy the graph and show these data included.

   b. With these new data included, does the median change or stay the same? Explain your reasoning.

Go Online
PHSchool.com

For: Multiple-Choice Skills
Practice
Web Code: ama-8154

For Exercises 14–20, tell whether the answers to the questions are numerical or categorical data.

14. What is your height in centimeters?

15. What is your favorite musical group?

16. What would you like to do after you graduate from high school?

17. Are students in Mr. Perez's class older than students in Ms. Sato's class?

18. What kind(s) of transportation do you use to get to school?

19. How much time do you spend doing homework?

20. On a scale of 1 to 7, with 7 being outstanding and 1 being poor, how would you rate the cafeteria food?

21. Use the graph for Name Lengths from Exercises 7–12. Make a horizontal bar graph of Ms. Campo's students' name length data.

   a. What is the median name length? How does it compare with the answer you found in Exercise 12? Why do you think this is so?

   b. A new student joins Ms. Campo's class. The student has a name length of 16 letters. Add this data value to your graph. Does the median change? Explain.

Connections

For Exercises 22–25, use the bar graphs below. The graphs show information about a class of middle-school students.

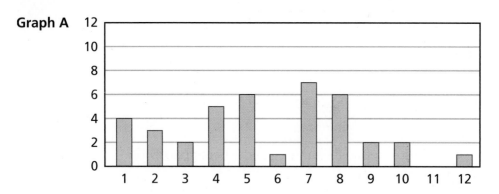

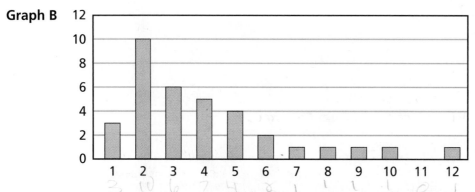

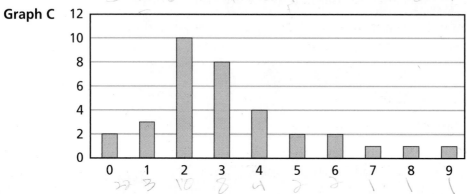

22. Which graph might show the number of children in the students' families? Explain.

23. Which graph might show the birth months of the students? Explain. **Hint:** Months are often written using numbers instead of names. For example, 1 means January, 2 means February, etc.

24. Which graph might show the number of toppings students like on their pizzas? Explain.

25. Give a possible title, a label for the vertical axis, and a label for the horizontal axis for each graph based on your answers to Exercises 22–24.

For Exercises 26–31, use the graph below. The graph shows the number of juice drinks 100 middle-school students consume in one day.

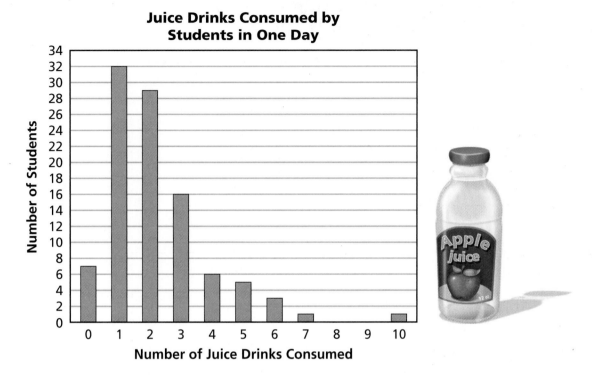

Juice Drinks Consumed by Students in One Day

26. A student used this graph to estimate that the median number of juice drinks students consume in a day is five. How can you tell that this estimate is not correct without finding the median?

27. Another student estimates that the median number of juice drinks is 1. Explain why the student is not correct.

28. **Multiple Choice** What is the range of these data?

    A. 9 drinks **B.** 10 drinks **C.** 11 drinks **D.** 12 drinks

29. **a.** What fraction of the students consumed two juice drinks?

    b. What percent of the students consumed three juice drinks?

30. What is the total number of juice drinks these 100 students consume in one day? How did you determine your answer?

31. Are these data numerical or categorical? Explain.

Homework Help Online
PHSchool.com
For: Help with Exercise 29
Web Code: ame-8129

32. Alex has a rat that is three years old. He wonders if his rat is old compared to other rats. At the pet store, he finds out that the median age for a rat is $2\frac{1}{2}$ years.

    a. What does the median tell Alex about the life span for a rat?

    b. How would knowing how the data vary from the least value to the greatest value help Alex predict the life span of his rat?

Extensions

For Exercises 33–39, use the bar graphs below.

A greeting card store sells stickers and street signs with first names on them. The store ordered 12 stickers and 12 street signs for each name. The table and the four bar graphs show the numbers of stickers and street signs that remain for the names that begin with the letter A.

Sales of Stickers and Street Signs

Name	Stickers Remaining	Street Signs Remaining
Aaron	1	9
Adam	2	7
Alicia	7	4
Allison	2	3
Amanda	0	11
Amber	2	3
Amy	3	3
Andrea	2	4
Andrew	8	6
Andy	3	5
Angela	8	4
Ana	10	7

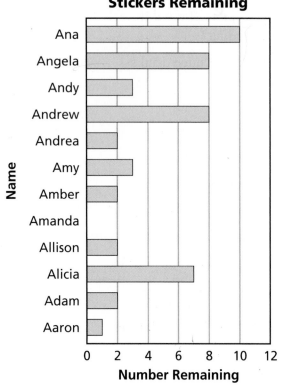

Graph A: Stickers Remaining

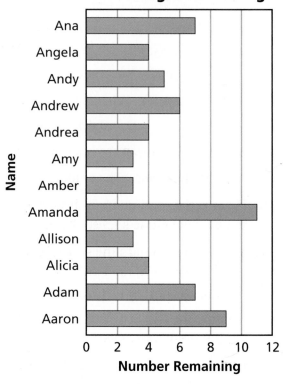

Graph B: Street Signs Remaining

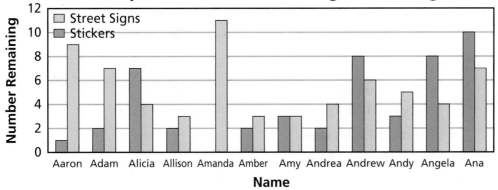

Graph C: Stickers and Street Signs Remaining

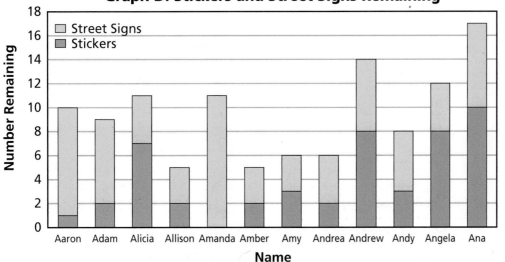

Graph D: Stickers and Street Signs Remaining

33. Use Graph A. How many Alicia stickers are left? How many Alicia stickers have been sold? Explain.

34. Use Graph B. How many Alicia street signs are left? How many Alicia street signs have been sold? Explain.

35. Are the stickers more popular than the street signs? Explain.

36. If each sticker costs $1.50, how much money has the store collected from selling name stickers for names beginning with the letter A?

37. For which name has the store sold the most stickers? For which name has the store sold the least stickers?

38. Graph C is a *double bar graph*. Use this graph to determine the name(s) for which the number of street signs sold and the number of stickers sold are the same.

39. Graph D is a *stacked bar graph*. Use this graph to determine whether some names are more popular than others. Justify your answer.

For Exercises 40–43, use the data below.

These data show the kinds of pets middle-school students have. From these data we cannot tell how many students were surveyed. We only know that 841 pets were counted.

**Kinds of Pets
Students Have**

Pet	Frequency
bird	61
cat	184
dog	180
fish	303
gerbil	17
guinea pig	12
hamster	32
horse	28
rabbit	2
snake	9
turtle	13
Total	**841**

40. Make a bar graph to display the distribution of these data. Think about how you will design and label the horizontal and vertical axes.

41. Use the information displayed in your graph to write a paragraph about the pets these students have. Compare these data with the data in Problem 1.4.

42. Jane said that close to 50% of the animals owned were birds, cats, or dogs. Do you agree or disagree? Explain.

43. What might be a good estimate of how many students were surveyed? (Use the data about number of pets each student had from Problem 1.4 to help you.) Explain.

Mathematical Reflections 1

In this investigation, you learned some ways to describe what is typical about a set of data. The following questions will help you summarize what you have learned.

Think about your answers to these questions. Discuss your ideas with other students and your teacher. Then write a summary of your findings in your notebook.

1. How are a table of data, a line plot, and a bar graph alike? How are they different?

2. What does the mode tell you about the distribution of a set of data? Can the mode be used to describe both categorical data and numerical data?

3. What does the median tell you about the distribution of a set of data? Can the median be used to describe both categorical data and numerical data?

4. Can the mode and the median of a set of data be the same values? Can they be different? Explain.

5. Why is it helpful to give the range when you describe the distribution of a set of data? Can the range be used to describe both categorical and numerical data?

6. How is the range of a set of data related to how the data vary from the least value to the greatest value?

7. How can you describe what is typical about the distribution of a set of data?

Unit Project   What's Next?

To carry out a research project about characteristics of the typical middle-school student, you will need to pose questions. What questions might you ask that would have categorical data as answers? What questions might you ask that have numerical data as answers? How would you display the information you gather about each of these questions? Write your thoughts in your notebook.

Using Graphs to Explore Data

Sometimes data may be spread out. When these data are displayed on a line plot or a bar graph, it is not easy to see patterns. In this investigation, you will learn how to highlight data using displays called stem-and-leaf plots and back-to-back stem-and-leaf plots to help you see patterns.

In Investigation 1, you analyzed single sets of data. Sometimes you may want to analyze whether there is a relationship between two different data sets. In this investigation, you will learn how to display data pairs from two different data sets using a coordinate graph.

2.1 Traveling to School

While investigating the times they got up in the morning, a middle-school class was surprised to find that two students got up almost an hour earlier than their classmates. These students said they got up early because it took them a long time to get to school. The class then wondered how much time it took each student to travel to school. The data they collected are on the next page.

Getting Ready for Problem 2.1

Use the table on the next page to answer these questions:

- What three questions did the students ask?
- How might the students have collected the travel-time data?
- Would a line plot be a good way to show the data? Why or why not?

Times and Distances to School

Student's Initials	Time (minutes)	Distance (miles)	Mode of Travel
DB	60	4.50	Bus
DD	15	2.00	Bus
CC	30	2.00	Bus
FH	35	2.50	Bus
SE	15	0.75	Car
AE	15	1.00	Bus
CL	15	1.00	Bus
LM	22	2.00	Bus
QN	25	1.50	Bus
MP	20	1.50	Bus
AP	25	1.25	Bus
AP	19	2.25	Bus
HCP	15	1.50	Bus
KR	8	0.25	Walking
NS	8	1.25	Car
LS	5	0.50	Bus
AT	20	2.75	Bus
JW	15	1.50	Bus
DW	17	2.50	Bus
SW	15	2.00	Car
NW	10	0.50	Walking
JW	20	0.50	Walking
CW	15	2.25	Bus
BA	30	3.00	Bus
JB	20	2.50	Bus
AB	50	4.00	Bus
BB	30	4.75	Bus
MB	20	2.00	Bus
RC	10	1.25	Bus
CD	5	0.25	Walking
ME	5	0.50	Bus
CF	20	1.75	Bus
KG	15	1.75	Bus
TH	11	1.50	Bus
EL	6	1.00	Car
KLD	35	0.75	Bus
MN	17	4.50	Bus
JO	10	3.00	Car
RP	21	1.50	Bus
ER	10	1.00	Bus

The students decide to make a stem-and-leaf plot of the travel times.

A **stem-and-leaf plot** looks like a vertical stem with leaves to the right of it. It is sometimes simply called a *stem plot*.

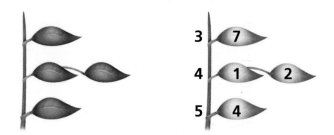

To make a stem plot to represent travel times, separate each data value into a left "stem" and a right "leaf."

For these data, the "stem" will be the tens digits. Because the travel times include values from 5 minutes to 60 minutes, the stem will be the digits 0, 1, 2, 3, 4, 5, and 6.

- Make a vertical list of the tens digits in order from least to greatest.

- Draw a line to the right of the digits to separate the stem from the "leaves."

```
0 |
1 |
2 |
3 |
4 |
5 |
6 |
```

The "leaves" will be the ones digits. For each data value, add a leaf next to the appropriate tens digit on the stem.

- The first data value is 60 minutes. Write a 0 next to the stem of 6.

- The next value is 15 minutes. Write a 5 next to the stem of 1.

- The travel times of 30 and 35 minutes are shown by a 0 and 5 next to the stem of 3.

```
0 |
1 | 5
2 |
3 | 0 5
4 |
5 |
6 | 0
```

A. Use the Travel to School data to make the stem plot. The plot is started for you.

```
0 |
1 | 5 5 5 5
2 | 2 5 0
3 | 0 5
4 |
5 |
6 | 0
```

B. Now redraw the stem plot, putting the data in each leaf in order from least to greatest. Include a title for your plot. Also include a key like the following that tells how to read the plot.

Key
2 | 5 means 25 minutes

C. Which students probably get to sleep the latest in the morning? Why do you think this?

D. Which students probably get up the earliest? Why do you think this?

E. What is the median of the travel-time data? Explain how you found this.

F. What is the range of the travel-time data? Explain.

ACE Homework starts on page 40.

Mrs. Reid's class competed against Mr. Costo's class in a jump-rope contest. Each student jumped as many times as possible. Another student counted the jumps and recorded the total. The classes made the *back-to-back stem plot* shown to display their data. Look at this plot carefully. Try to figure out how to read it.

When the two classes compare their results, they disagree about which class did better.

- Mr. Costo's class says that the range of their data is much greater.

- Mrs. Reid's class says this is only because they had one person who jumped many more times than anybody else.

- Mrs. Reid's class claims that most of them jumped more times than most of the students in Mr. Costo's class.

- Mr. Costo's class argues that even if they do not count the person with 300 jumps, they still did better.

Number of Jumps

Mrs. Reid's class		Mr. Costo's class
8 7 7 7 5 1 1	0	1 1 2 3 4 5 8 8
6 1 1	1	0 7
9 7 6 3 0 0	2	3 7 8
7 6 5 3	3	0 3 5
5 0	4	2 7 8
	5	0 2 3
2	6	0 8
	7	
9 8 0	8	
6 3 1	9	
	10	2 4
3	11	
	12	
	13	
	14	
	15	1
	16	0 0
	17	
	18	
	19	
	20	
	21	
	22	
	23	
	24	
	25	
	26	
	27	
	28	
	29	
	30	0

Key: 7 | 3 | 0 means 37 jumps for Mrs. Reid's class and 30 jumps for Mr. Costo's class

A. Which class did better overall in the jump-rope contest? Use what you know about statistics to help you justify your answer.

B. In Mr. Costo's class, there are some very large numbers of jumps. For example, one student jumped 151 times, and another student jumped 300 times. We call these data outliers. **Outliers** are data values that are located far from the rest of the other values in a set of data. Find two other outliers in the data for Mr. Costo's class.

C. An outlier may be a value that was recorded incorrectly, or it may be a signal that something special is happening. All the values recorded for Mr. Costo's class are correct. What might account for the few students who jumped many more times than their classmates?

ACE | Homework starts on page 40.

In earlier problems, you worked with one measure at a time. For example, you looked at the number of letters in students' names and travel times to school. In this problem, you will look at the relationship between two different counts or measures.

If you look around at your classmates, you might guess that taller people have wider arm spans. But is there *really* any relationship between a person's height and his or her arm span? The best way to find out more about this question is to collect some data.

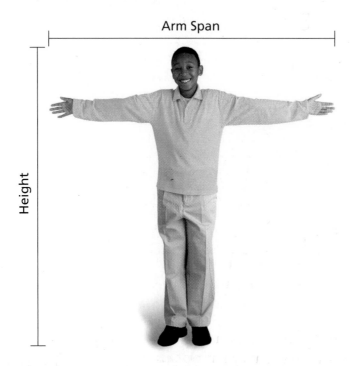

Here are data on height and arm span (measured from fingertip to fingertip) that one class collected.

Height and Arm Span Measurements

Initials	Height (inches)	Arm Span (inches)
NY	63	60
JJ	69	67
CM	73	75
PL	77	77
BP	64	65
AS	67	64
KR	58	58

You can show two different data values at the same time on a **coordinate graph.** Each point on a coordinate graph represents two data values. The horizontal axis, or *x*-axis, represents one data value. The vertical axis, or *y*-axis, represents a second data value. The graph below shows data for height along the *x*-axis and data for arm span along the *y*-axis. Each point on the graph represents the height and the arm span for one student.

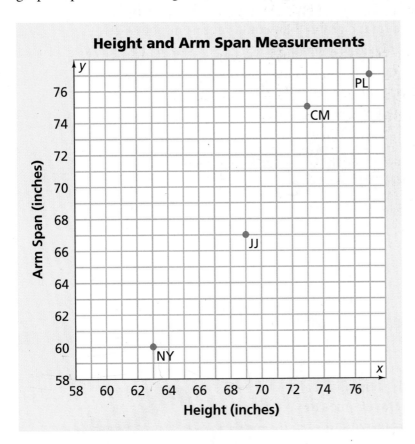

Study the table of data on the previous page and the coordinate graph. Four points have already been plotted and labeled with the students' initials. The location of each point is shown in the table at the right.

Initials	Point
NY	(63, 60)
JJ	(69, 67)
CM	(73, 75)
PL	(77, 77)

Getting Ready for Problem

- Where would you place the points and initials for the remaining three people?
- Why do the axes of the graph start at (58, 58)?
- What would the graph look like if the axes started at (0, 0)?

Problem 2.3 Making and Reading Coordinate Graphs

Collect the height and arm span data of each person in your class. Make a coordinate graph of your data. Use the graph to answer the questions.

A. If you know the measure of a person's arm span, do you know his or her height? Explain.

B. Draw a diagonal line on the graph that would represent points at which arm span and height are equal.

   1. How many data points lie on this line? How does arm span relate to height for the points *on* the line?

   2. How many data points lie below this line? How does arm span relate to height for the points *below* the line?

   3. How many data points lie above this line? How does arm span relate to height for the points *above* the line?

ACE **Homework starts on page 40.**

2.4 Relating Travel Time to Distance

In Problem 2.1, you made stem-and-leaf plots to show data about travel times to school. You can use the same data to look at the relationship between travel time and distance from home to school on a coordinate graph.

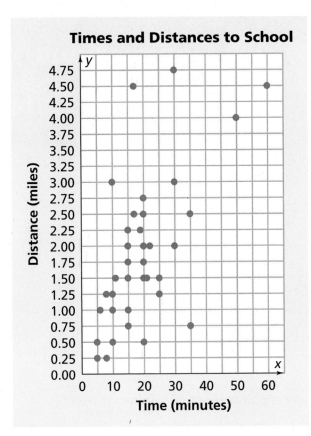

Times and Distances to School

Distance (miles) vs. Time (minutes)

Problem 2.4 Using Coordinate Graphs to Find Relationships

Study the graph above and the data from Problem 2.1.

A. Copy the coordinate graph. Mark and label a point with the student's initial for the first five students in the table.

B. If you know a student's travel time, what do you know about that student's distance from school? Use the graph to justify your answer.

C. Locate each set of points on the coordinate graph. What can you tell about travel time and distance from school for the students these points represent?

　1. (17, 4.50) and (60, 4.50)

　2. (30, 2.00), (30, 3.00), and (30, 4.75)

　3. (17, 4.50) and (30, 4.75)

D. 1. Why do the axes have different scales?

　2. What would the graph look like if both axes used the same scales?

For: Statistical Tool
Visit: PHSchool.com
Web Code: amd-8204

ACE Homework starts on page 40.

Applications

For Exercises 1–4, use the stem-and-leaf plot at the right.

Student Travel Times to School

0	3 3 5 7 8 9
1	0 2 3 5 6 6 8 9
2	0 1 3 3 3 5 5 8 8
3	0 5
4	5

Key: 2 | 5 means 25 min

1. **Multiple Choice** How many students spent 10 minutes traveling to school?

   A. 1   **B.** 9   **C.** 10   **D.** 19

2. **Multiple Choice** How many students spent 15 minutes or more traveling to school?

   F. 10   **G.** 16   **H.** 17   **J.** 25

3. How many students are in the class? Explain.

4. What is the typical time it took these students to travel to school? Explain.

For Exercises 5–8, use the table on the next page.

5. Make a stem-and-leaf plot of the students' ages. The plot has been started for you at the right. Notice that the first value in the stem is 6, because there are no values less than 60 months.

6. What ages, in years, does the interval of 80–89 months represent?

7. What is the median age of these students?

8. **a.** On a piece of grid paper, make a coordinate graph. Show age (in months) on the horizontal axis and height (in centimeters) on the vertical axis. To help you choose a scale for each axis, look at the least and greatest values for each measure.

   b. Explain how you can use your graph to find out whether the youngest student is also the shortest student.

6
7
8
9
10
11
12
13
14
15

c. Use your graph to describe what happens to students' heights as the students get older.

d. What would happen to the graph if you extended it to include people in their late teens or early twenties? Explain.

Student Ages, Heights, and Foot Lengths

Age (mo)	Height (cm)	Foot Length (cm)	Age (mo)	Height (cm)	Foot Length (cm)
76	126	24	148	164	26
73	117	24	140	152	22
68	112	17	114	135	20
78	123	22	108	135	22
81	117	20	105	147	22
82	122	23	113	138	22
80	130	22	120	141	20
90	127	21	120	146	24
101	127	21	132	147	23
99	124	21	132	155	21
103	130	20	129	141	22
101	134	21	138	161	28
145	172	32	152	156	30
146	163	27	149	157	27
144	158	25	132	150	25

9. The coordinate graph below shows the height and foot length data from the table on the previous page. Notice that the scale on the *x*-axis uses intervals of 5 centimeters and the scale on the *y*-axis uses intervals of 1 centimeter.

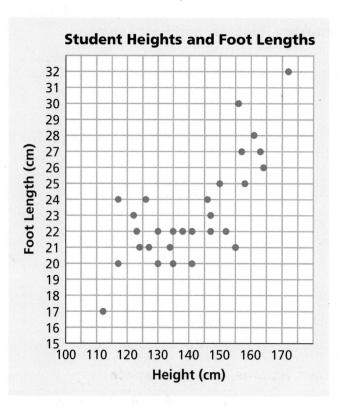

a. If you know a person's foot length, can you tell that person's height? Explain.

b. Find the median height and the median foot length. The median height is about how many times the median foot length?

c. Measure the length of your foot in centimeters. Your height is about how many times your foot length?

d. Look at your responses to parts (b) and (c). How can you use this information to answer part (a)? Explain.

e. What would the graph look like if you started each axis at 0?

Connections

10. a. Use the data in the Student Ages, Heights, and Foot Lengths table from Exercises 5–8. Make a stem-and-leaf plot of the students' heights.

b. Describe how to make a line plot of the students' heights. What are the least and greatest data values? How does this help you make the line plot?

c. Describe how to make a bar graph of the students' heights. What are the least and greatest data values? How does this help you make the graph?

d. Why might you display these data using a stem-and-leaf plot instead of a line plot or a bar graph?

11. The table below shows some of the Student Ages, Heights, and Foot Lengths data in centimeters. The table includes two new columns. Copy and complete the table to show heights and foot lengths in meters.

a. Round the height for each student to the nearest tenth of a meter.

b. Make a line plot showing these rounded height data.

c. What is the typical height for these students in meters? Explain.

Homework Help Online
PHSchool.com

For: Help with Exercise 11
Web Code: ame-8211

Student Ages, Heights, and Foot Lengths

Age (mo)	Height (cm)	Height (m)	Foot Length (cm)	Foot Length (m)
76	126	▦	24	▦
73	117	▦	24	▦
68	112	▦	17	▦
78	123	▦	22	▦
81	117	▦	20	▦
82	122	▦	23	▦
80	130	▦	22	▦
90	127	▦	21	▦
138	161	▦	28	▦
152	156	▦	30	▦
149	157	▦	27	▦
132	150	▦	25	▦

12. The pie chart shows the portion of time Harold spent on homework in each subject last week.

Time Spent on Homework

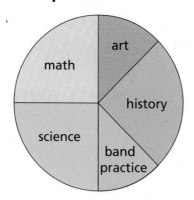

a. If Harold spent two hours on math homework, about how many hours did he spend on homework altogether?

b. About what percent of his time did Harold spend on math, science, and history homework? Explain.

Extensions

For Exercises 13 and 14, use the jump-rope data on the next page.

13. Make a back-to-back stem-and-leaf plot that compares either the girls in Mrs. Reid's class with the girls in Mr. Costo's class or the boys in Mrs. Reid's class with the boys in Mr. Costo's class. Did the girls (or boys) in one class do better than the girls (or boys) in the other class? Explain your reasoning.

14. Make a back-to-back stem-and-leaf plot that compares the girls in both classes with the boys in both classes. Did the girls do better than the boys? Explain.

Number of Jumps

Mrs. Reid's Class Data		Mr. Costo's Class Data	
Boy	5	Boy	1
Boy	35	Boy	30
Girl	91	Boy	28
Boy	62	Boy	10
Girl	96	Girl	27
Girl	23	Girl	102
Boy	16	Boy	47
Boy	1	Boy	8
Boy	8	Girl	160
Boy	11	Girl	23
Girl	93	Boy	17
Girl	27	Boy	2
Girl	88	Girl	68
Boy	26	Boy	50
Boy	7	Girl	151
Boy	7	Boy	60
Boy	1	Boy	5
Boy	40	Girl	52
Boy	7	Girl	4
Boy	20	Girl	35
Girl	20	Boy	160
Girl	89	Boy	1
Boy	29	Boy	3
Boy	11	Boy	8
Boy	113	Girl	48
Boy	33	Boy	42
Girl	45	Boy	33
Girl	80	Girl	300
Boy	36	Girl	104
Girl	37	Girl	53

15. A group of students challenged each other to see who could come the closest to guessing the number of seeds in his or her pumpkin. The data they collected are shown in the table and the graph.

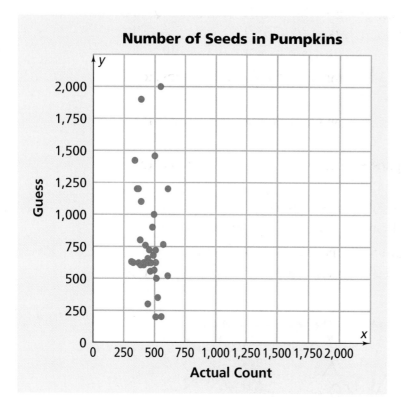

Number of Seeds in Pumpkins

Guess	Actual
630	309
621	446
801	381
720	505
1,900	387
1,423	336
621	325
1,200	365
622	410
1,000	492
1,200	607
1,458	498
350	523
621	467
759	423
900	479
500	512
521	606
564	494
655	441
722	455
202	553
621	367
300	442
200	507
556	462
604	384
2,000	545
1,200	354
766	568
624	506
680	486
605	408
1,100	387

a. What do you notice about how the actual counts vary? What are the median and the least and greatest values of the actual counts?

b. What do you notice about how the guesses vary? What are the median and the least and greatest values of the guesses?

c. Make your own coordinate graph of the data. Draw a diagonal line on the graph to connect the points (0, 0), (250, 250), (500, 500), all the way to (2,250, 2,250).

d. What is true about the guesses compared to the actual counts for points near the line you drew?

e. What is true about the guesses compared to the actual counts for points above the line?

f. What is true about the guesses compared to the actual counts for points below the line?

g. In general, did the students make good guesses? Use what you know about median and range to explain your reasoning.

h. The scales on the axes are the same, but the data are bunched together. How would you change the scale to show the data points better?

Mathematical Reflections 2

In this investigation, you learned how to make stem-and-leaf plots as a way to group a set of data so you can study its shape. You have also learned how to make and read coordinate graphs. Coordinate graphs let you examine two things at once so you can look for relationships between them. The following questions will help you summarize what you have learned.

Think about your answers to these questions. Discuss your ideas with other students and your teacher. Then write a summary of your findings in your notebook.

1. Describe how to locate the median and range using a stem plot.

2. When you make a coordinate graph of data pairs, how do you determine where to place each point?

3. What do you consider when choosing a scale for each axis of a coordinate graph?

4. Numerical data can be displayed using more than one kind of graph. How do you decide when to use a line plot, a bar graph, a stem-and-leaf plot, or a coordinate graph?

Unit Project What's Next?

Think about the survey you will be conducting about middle-school students. What kinds of questions can you ask that might involve using a stem-and-leaf plot to display the data? Can you sort your data into two groups and use a back-to-back stem plot to help you compare the data?

What Do We Mean by *Mean?*

The main use of the United States Census is to find out how many people live in the United States. The census provides useful information about household size. In the census, the term *household* means all the people who live in a "housing unit" (such as a house, an apartment, or a room of a boarding house).

In earlier investigations, you used median and mode to describe a set of data. Another measure of center is the *mean*. It is the most commonly used measure of center for numerical data. Another word often used to indicate the mean of a set of data is *average*.

Finding the Mean

Six students in a middle-school class use the United States Census guidelines to find the number of people in their household. Each student then makes a stack of cubes to show the number of people in his or her household.

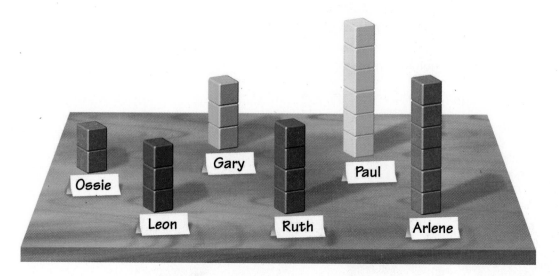

You can see from the stacks that the six households vary in size.

Getting Ready for Problem 3.1

Use cubes and make stacks like the ones shown above. Use the stacks to answer these questions:

- What is the median of these data?
- What is the mode of these data?

Make the stacks all the same height by moving cubes.

- How many cubes are in each stack?
- The average stack height you found represents the mean number of people in a household. What is the mean number of people in a household?

Another group of students made the table below.

Household Size

Name	Number of People
Reggie	6
Tara	4
Brendan	3
Felix	4
Hector	3
Tonisha	4

A. Make stacks of cubes to show the size of each household.

   1. How many people are in the six households altogether? Explain.

   2. What is the mean number of people per household? Explain.

   3. How does the mean for these data compare to the mean for the data in the Getting Ready?

B. What are some ways to determine the mean number of a set of data other than using cubes?

ACE Homework starts on page 56.

The line plots below show two different distributions with the same mean.

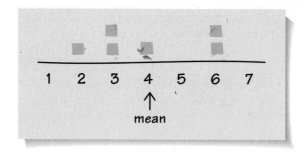

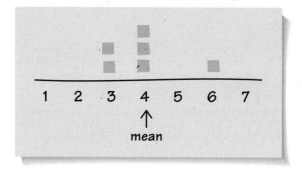

Getting Ready for Problem 3.2

- How many households are there in each situation?
- What is the total number of people in each situation?
- How do these facts relate to the mean in each case?

A. Find two new data sets for six households that each has a mean of 4 people per household. Use cubes to show each data set. Then make line plots from the cubes.

B. Find two different data sets for seven households that each has a mean of 4 people per household. Use cubes to show each set. Then make line plots from the cubes.

C. A group of seven students find they have a mean of 3 people per household. Find a data set that fits this description. Then make a line plot for this data.

D. 1. A group of six students has a mean of $3\frac{1}{2}$ people per household. Find a data set that fits this description. Then make a line plot for this data.

2. How can the mean be $3\frac{1}{2}$ people when "half" a person does not exist?

3. How can you predict when the mean number of people per household will not be a whole number?

ACE **Homework starts on page 56.**

A group of middle-school students answered the question: How many movies did you watch last month? The table and stem plot show their data.

Movies Watched

Student	Number
Joel	15
Tonya	16
Rachel	5
Swanson	18
Jerome	3
Leah	6
Beth	7
Mickey	6
Bhavana	3
Josh	11

Movies Watched

```
0 | 3 3 5 6 6 7
1 | 1 5 6 8
2 |
```
Key: 1 | 5 means 15 movies

You have found the mean using cubes to represent the data. You may know the following procedure to find the mean: The **mean** of a set of data is the sum of the values divided by the number of values in the set.

Problem 3.3 Using the Mean

A. Use the movie data to find each number.

1. the total number of students

2. the total number of movies watched

3. the mean number of movies watched

B. A new value is added for Carlos, who was home last month with a broken leg. He watched 31 movies.

1. How does the new value change the distribution on the stem plot?

2. Is this new value an outlier? Explain.

3. What is the mean of the data now?

4. Compare the mean from Question A to the new mean. What do you notice? Explain.

C. Data for eight more students are added:

Tommy	5	Robbie	4
Alexandra	5	Ana	4
Trevor	5	Alicia	2
Kirsten	4	Brian	2

1. How do these values change the distribution on the stem plot?

2. Are any of these new data values outliers? Explain.

3. What is the mean of the data now?

4. Compare the means you found in Questions A and B with this new mean. What do you notice? Explain.

D. 1. What happens to the mean of a data set when you add one or more data values that are outliers? Explain.

2. What happens to the mean of a data set when you add data values that cluster near one end of the original data set? Explain.

3. Explain why you think these changes might occur.

ACE **Homework starts on page 56.**

Applications

For Exercises 1 and 2, use the line plot.

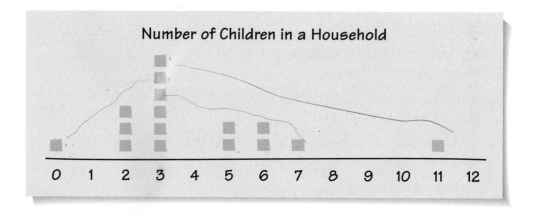

Number of Children in a Household

0 1 2 3 4 5 6 7 8 9 10 11 12

1. a. What is the median number of children for the 16 households? Explain how to find the median. What does the median tell you?

   b. Do any of the 16 households have the median number of children? Explain.

2. a. What is the mean number of children per household for the 16 households? Explain how to find the mean. What does the mean tell you?

   b. Do any of the 16 households have the mean number of children? Explain.

For Exercises 3 and 4, the mean number of people per household for eight households is 6 people.

3. Multiple Choice What is the total number of people in the eight households?

   A. 11   **B.** 16   **C.** 48   **D.** 64

4. a. Make a line plot showing one possible arrangement for the numbers of people in the eight households.

   b. Make a line plot showing a different possible arrangement for the numbers of people in the eight households.

   c. Are the medians the same for the two arrangements you made?

Go Online
PHSchool.com
For: Multiple-Choice Skills
Web Code: ama-8354

5. A group of nine students has a mean of $3\frac{1}{3}$ people per household. Make a line plot showing a data set that fits this description.

6. A group of nine students has a mean of 5 people per household. The largest household in the group has 10 people. Make a line plot showing a data set that fits this description.

Connections

7. The students in Mr. Wilson's study hall spent the following amounts of time on their homework.

   $\frac{3}{4}$ hour $\frac{1}{2}$ hour $1\frac{1}{4}$ hours $\frac{3}{4}$ hour $\frac{1}{2}$ hour

   What is the mean time his students spent on homework?

8. **Multiple Choice** Use the data from Exercise 7. What is the median time Mr. Wilson's students spent on homework?

   F. $\frac{1}{2}$ hour   **G.** $\frac{3}{4}$ hour   **H.** 1 hour   **J.** $1\frac{1}{4}$ hour

9. A soccer league wants to find the average amount of water the players drink per game. There are 18 players on a team and 10 teams in the league. The players drank a total of 5,760 ounces of water during one day in which each team played exactly one game.

   a. How much water did each player drink per game if they each drank the same amount of water?

   b. Does this value represent the mean or the median? Explain.

10. A grocery store carries nine different brands of granola bars. What are possible prices for the nine brands if the mean price is $2.66? Explain. You may use pictures to help you.

11. Ralph has a pet rabbit that is 5 years old. He wonders if his rabbit is old compared to other rabbits. He finds out that the mean life span for a rabbit is 7 years.

    a. What does the mean tell Ralph about the life span for a rabbit?

    b. What additional information would help Ralph to predict the life span of his rabbit?

12. Sabrina, Diego, and Marcus entered a dance contest that ran from 9 a.m. to 7 p.m. Below are the times that each student danced.

Homework
Help **Online**
PHSchool.com
For: Help with Exercise 12
Web Code: ame-8312

Dance Contest Schedule

Student	Time
Sabrina	9:15 a.m. to 1:00 p.m.
Diego	1:00 p.m. to 4:45 p.m.
Marcus	4:45 p.m. to 7:00 p.m.

    a. Write the time each student spent dancing as a mixed number.

    b. Look at the data from part (a). Without doing any computations, do you think the mean time spent dancing is the same as, less than, or greater than the median? Explain your reasoning.

For Exercises 13–16, a recent time study of 3,000 children ages 2–18 years old was conducted. The data are in the table below.

How Children Spend Their Time

Activity	Time (minutes per day)
Watching videos	39
Reading for fun	44
Using the computer for fun	21

13. Did each child watch videos for 39 minutes per day? Explain.

14. Thelma decides to round 39 minutes to 40 minutes. Then she estimates that children spend about $\frac{2}{3}$ of an hour watching videos. What percent of an hour is $\frac{2}{3}$?

15. Estimate what part of an hour children spend reading for fun. Write your answer as a fraction and as a decimal.

16. Children use a computer for fun for about 20 minutes per day. How many hours do they spend using a computer for fun in 1 week (7 days)? Write your answer as a fraction and as a decimal.

17. Three candidates are running for mayor of Slugville. Each has determined the typical income for the people in Slugville, using this information to help in their campaigns.

Mayor Phillips is running for re-election. He says, "Slugville is doing great! The average income for each person is $2,000 per week!"

Candidate Lily Jackson says, "Slugville is nice, but it needs my help! The average income is only $100 per week."

Candidate Ronnie Ruis says, "Slugville is in a lot of trouble! The average income is $0 per week."

Some of the candidates are confused about "average." Slugville has only 16 residents, and their weekly incomes are $0, $0, $0, $0, $0, $0, $0, $0, $200, $200, $200, $200, $200, $200, $200, and $30,600.

a. Explain which measure of center each of the candidates used as an "average" income for the town. Check their computations.

b. Does any person in Slugville have the mean income? Explain.

c. Does any person in Slugville have an income that equals the median? Explain.

d. Does any person in Slugville have an income that equals the mode? Explain.

e. What do you consider to be the typical income for a resident of Slugville? Explain.

f. Suppose four more people move to Slugville. Each has a weekly income of $200. How would the mean, median, and mode change?

18. A recent survey asked 25 middle-school students how many movies they watch in one month. The data are shown below. Notice that the data varies from 1 to 30 movies.

Movies Watched

Student	Number
Wes	2
Tomi	15
Ling	13
Su Chin	1
Michael	9
Mara	30
Alan	20
Jo	1
Tanisha	25
Susan	4
Gil	3
Enrique	2
Lonnie	3
Ken	10
Kristina	15
Mario	12
Henry	5
Julian	2
Alana	4
Tyrone	1
Rebecca	4
Anton	11
Jun	8
Raymond	8
Angelica	17

a. Make a stem-and-leaf plot to show these data. Describe the shape of the data.

b. Find the mean number of movies watched by the students. Explain.

c. What do the mean and how the data vary tell you about the typical number of movies watched for this group of students?

d. Find the median number of movies watched. Are the mean and the median the same? Why do you think this is so?

19. Six students each had a different number of pens. They put them all together and then distributed them so that each student had the same number of pens.

   a. Choose any of the following that could be the number of pens they had altogether. Explain your reasoning.

      A. 12   **B.** 18   **C.** 46   **D.** 48

   b. Use your response from part (a). How many pens did each person have after the pens were distributed evenly?

   c. Your classmate says that finding the mean number of pens per person is the same as finding the number of pens each person had after the pens were distributed evenly. Do you agree or disagree? Explain.

Extensions

For Exercises 20 and 21, use the newspaper headline.

20. Do you think that this headline is referring to a mean, a median, or something else? Explain.

21. About how many hours per day does the average third grader watch television if he or she watches 1,170 hours in a year?

22. Review the jump-rope data from Problem 2.2.

   a. What are the median and the mean for each class's data? How do the median and the mean compare for each class?

   b. Should Mr. Costo's class use the median or the mode to compare their performance with Mrs. Reid's class? Why?

   c. What happens to the median of Mr. Costo's class data if you leave out the data for the student who jumped rope 300 times? Why does this happen?

   d. What happens to the mean of Mr. Costo's class data if you leave out the data for the student who jumped rope 300 times? Why does this happen?

   e. Can Mrs. Reid's class claim they did better if Mr. Costo's class leaves out the data of 300 jumps? Explain.

23. A group of middle-school students answered the question: How many TV shows did you watch last week? The table at the right shows their data.

   a. Use the data to find the mean number of TV shows watched.

   b. A new value is added for Albert. He watched only 1 TV show last week.

   i. Is this new value an outlier?

   ii. What is the mean of the data now?

   iii. Compare this mean to the mean you found in part (a). What do you notice? Explain.

Student	Number of TV Shows Watched
Caleb	17
Malek	13
Jenna	20
Mario	8
Melania	11
Bennett	13
Anna	16

Mathematical Reflections 3

In this investigation, you have explored a type of measure of center called the mean. It is important to understand this mean, or average, and to relate it to the mode and the median. The following questions will help you summarize what you have learned.

Think about your answers to these questions. Discuss your ideas with other students and your teacher. Then write a summary of your findings in your notebook.

1. Describe a method for calculating mean. Explain why this method works.

2. You have used three measures of center: mode, median, and mean.

   a. Why do you suppose they are called "measures of center"?

   b. What does each tell you about a set of data?

   c. Why might you use the median instead of the mean?

3. You have also used range and how data vary from least to greatest values to describe data. Why might you use these with a measure of center to describe a data set?

4. Once you collect data to answer questions, you must decide what statistics you can use to describe your data.

   a. One student says you can only use the mode to describe categorical data, but you can use the mode, median, and mean to describe numerical data. Is the student correct? Explain.

   b. Can you find range for categorical data? Explain.

Unit Project | What's Next?

For your project for the unit, you are developing your own survey to gather information about middle-school students. What statistics can you use to describe the data you might collect for each question in your survey?

Unit Project

Is Anyone Typical?

You can use what you have learned in *Data About Us* to conduct a statistical investigation. Answer the question, "What are some characteristics of a typical middle-school student?" Complete your data collection, analysis, and interpretation. Then make a poster, write a report, or find some other way to display your results.

Your statistical investigation should consist of four parts:

- Asking Questions

  Decide what information you want to gather. You will want to gather both numerical data and categorical data. Your data may include physical characteristics, family characteristics, behaviors (such as hobbies), and preferences or opinions.

  Once you have decided what you want to know, write clear and appropriate questions. Everyone who takes your survey should interpret your questions the same way. For some questions, you may want to give answer choices. For example, instead of asking, "What is your favorite movie?" you could ask, "Which of the following movies do you like best?" and list several choices.

- Collecting the Data

  You can collect data from just your class or from a larger group of students. Decide how to distribute and collect the survey.

- Analyzing the Data

  Once you have collected your data, organize, display, and analyze them. Think about what types of displays and which measures of center are most appropriate for each set of data values you collect.

- Interpreting the Results

  Use the results of your analysis to describe some characteristics of the typical middle-school student. Is there a student that fits all the "typical" characteristics you found? If not, explain why.

Looking Back and Looking Ahead

Working on the problems in this unit, you explored some of the big ideas involved in conducting statistical investigations. You learned how to

- use a process of statistical investigation to pose questions, collect and analyze data, and interpret results
- represent data using bar graphs, line plots, stem-and-leaf plots, and coordinate graphs
- explore ways of using statistics such as mean, median, mode, and range to describe what is "typical" about data
- develop a variety of ways to compare data sets

Go Online
PHSchool.com

For: Vocabulary Review Puzzle
Web Code: amj-8051

Use Your Understanding: Statistical Reasoning

Naturalists in their studies of wild animal populations often use statistical reasoning. The data in the table on the next page show the lengths (in inches) and weights (in pounds) of 25 alligators captured in central Florida.

Lengths and Weights of Captured Alligators

Gator Number	Length (inches)	Weight (pounds)	Gator Number	Length (inches)	Weight (pounds)
1	74	54	14	88	70
2	94	110	15	58	28
3	85	84	16	90	102
4	61	44	17	94	130
5	128	366	18	68	39
6	72	61	19	78	57
7	89	84	20	86	80
8	90	106	21	72	38
9	63	33	22	74	51
10	82	80	23	147	640
11	114	197	24	76	42
12	69	36	25	86	90
13	86	83			

1. Consider the lengths of the alligators in the sample.

   a. Make a graph of the lengths of the 25 alligators. Describe the distribution of lengths in the graph.

   b. What are the mean and median lengths? Which might you use to describe the typical length of an alligator?

   c. What are the range and the least and greatest values of the lengths?

2. Consider the weights of alligators in the sample.

   a. Make a graph of the weights of the 25 alligators. Describe the distribution of weights in the graph.

   b. What are the mean and median weights? Which might you use to describe the typical weight of an alligator?

   c. What are the range and the least and greatest values of the weights?

3. **a.** Make a coordinate graph of the (*length, weight*) data.

   b. What do you notice about the relationship between length and weight of alligators in the sample that are

      i. 61 and 63 inches long?   **ii.** 82, 85, and 86 inches long?

      iii. 90, 94, and 114 inches long?

   c. What weight would you predict for an alligator that is

      i. 70 inches long?   **ii.** 100 inches long?

      iii. 130 inches long?

   d. Do you believe it is possible to make a good estimate for the weight of an alligator if you know its length?

Explain Your Reasoning

When you describe a collection of data, you look for the shape of the distribution of the data. You can often visualize data patterns using graphs.

4. How do the mean and the median help in describing the distribution of data in a data set?

5. How do the range and how data vary from least to greatest values help in describing the distribution of data in a data set?

6. How do you know when to use each graph to display numerical data?

   a. line plots   **b.** stem-and-leaf plots   **c.** coordinate graphs

7. What does it mean to say that a person's arm span *is related to* his or her height, or that the weight of an alligator *is related to* its length?

Look Ahead

The ideas about statistics and data analysis that you have learned in this unit will be used and extended in a variety of future *Connected Mathematics* units. In *Data Distributions*, you will explore how data vary and ways to compare data sets. In *Samples and Populations*, you will explore sampling, comparing samples, and comparing different variables in a sample. You'll also find that various statistical plots and data summaries appear in everyday news reports and in the technical work of science, business, and government.

English / Spanish Glossary

B

bar graph (bar chart) A graphical representation of a table of data in which the height or length of each bar indicates its frequency. The bars are separated from each other to highlight that the data are discrete or "counted" data. In a vertical bar graph, the horizontal axis shows the values or categories, and the vertical axis shows the frequency or tally for each of the values or categories on the horizontal axis. In a horizontal bar graph, the vertical axis shows the values or categories, and the horizontal axis shows the frequencies.

gráfica de barras (tabla de barras) Representación gráfica de una tabla de datos en la que la altura o longitud de cada barra indica su frecuencia. Las barras están separadas entre sí para subrayar que los datos son discretos o "contados". En una gráfica de barras vertical, el eje horizontal representa los valores o categorías, y el eje vertical representa la frecuencia o el cómputo de cada uno de los valores o categorías en el eje horizontal. En una gráfica de barras horizontal, el eje vertical representa los valores o categorías, y el eje horizontal representa las frecuencias.

Vertical Bar Graph

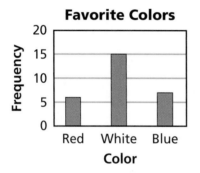

Horizontal Bar Graph

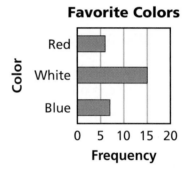

C

categorical data Data that are "words" that represent possible responses within a given category. Frequency counts can be made of the values for a given category. The table below shows examples of categories and their possible values.

datos categóricos Valores que son "palabras" que representan respuestas posibles en una categoría dada. Se pueden contar las frecuencias de los valores para una categoría dada. La siguiente tabla muestra ejemplos de categorías y sus posibles valores.

Category	Possible Values
Month people are born	January, February, March
Favorite color to wear	magenta, blue, yellow
Kinds of pets people have	cats, dogs, fish, horses

coordinate graph A graphical representation in which points are used to denote pairs of related numerical values. For each point, the two coordinates of the point give the associated numerical values in the appropriate order. Using the table below, the *x*-coordinate could represent height, and the *y*-coordinate could represent arm span. The coordinate graph would look like the one below the table.

gráfica de coordenadas Representación gráfica en la que se usan puntos para denotar los pares de valores numéricos relacionados. Para cada punto, las dos coordenadas del punto dan los valores numéricos asociados en el orden apropiado. En la tabla de abajo, la coordenada *x* podría representar la altura y la coordenada *y* podría representar la longitud del brazo. La gráfica de coordenada sería como la que está debajo de la tabla.

Height and Arm Span Measurements

Initials	Height (inches)	Arm Span (inches)
JJ	69	67
NY	63	60
CM	73	75
PL	77	77

Height and Arm Span Measurements

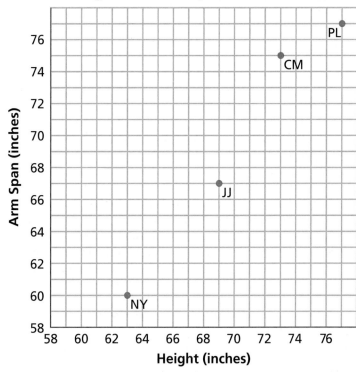

data Values such as counts, ratings, measurements, or opinions that are gathered to answer questions. The data in this table show mean temperatures in three cities.

datos Valores como cómputos, calificaciones, medidas u opiniones que se recogen para responder a preguntas. Los datos en esta tabla representan las temperaturas medias en tres ciudades.

Daily Mean Temperatures

City	Mean Temperature (°F)
Mobile, Ala.	67.5
Boston, Mass.	51.3
Spokane, Wash.	47.3

line plot A quick, simple way to organize data along a number line where the Xs (or other symbols) above a number represent how often each value is mentioned.

diagrama de puntos Una manera rápida y sencilla de organizar datos en una recta numérica donde las X (u otros símbolos) colocadas encima de un número representan la frecuencia con que se menciona cada valor.

Number of Siblings Students Have

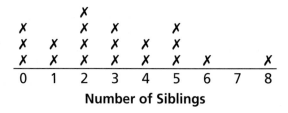

Number of Siblings

mean The value you would get if all the data are combined and then redistributed evenly. For example, the total number of siblings for the above data is 56 siblings. If all 19 students had the same number of siblings, they would each have about 3 siblings. Differences from the mean "balance out" so that the sum of differences below and above the mean equal 0. The mean of a set of data is the sum of the values divided by the number of values in the set.

media El valor se logra que si todos los datos se combinan y después se redistribuyen uniformemente. Por ejemplo, el número total de hermanos y hermanas para los datos en el diagrama de arriba es de 56. Si los 19 estudiantes tuvieran la misma cantidad de hermanos y hermanas, cada uno tendría aproximadamente 3 hermanos o hermanas. Las diferencias de la media se "equilibran" de tal manera que la suma de las diferencias por encima y por debajo de la media es igual a 0. La media de un conjunto de datos es la suma de los valores dividido por el número de valores en el conjunto.

median The number that marks the middle of an ordered set of data. At least half of the values lie at or above the median, and at least half lie at or below the median. The median of the distribution of siblings is 3 because the tenth (middle) value in the ordered set of 19 values (0, 0, 0, 1, 1, 2, 2, 2, 2, 3, 3, 3, 4, 4, 5, 5, 5, 6, 8) is 3 siblings.

mediana El número que señala la mitad en un conjunto ordenado de datos. Por lo menos mitad de los datos ocurre en o encima de la mediana, y por lo menos mitad de los datos ocurre en o debajo de la mediana. La mediana de la distribución de hermanos y hermanas es 3 porque el décimo valor (el del medio) en el conjunto ordenado de 19 valores (0, 0, 0, 1, 1, 2, 2, 2, 2, 3, 3, 3, 4, 4, 5, 5, 5, 6, 8) es 3 hermanos o hermanas.

mode The category or numerical value that occurs most often. The mode of the distribution of siblings is 2. It is possible for a set of data to have more than one mode.

moda En una distribución, es la categoría o el valor numérico que ocurre con mayor frecuencia. La moda de la distribución de hermanos o hermanas es 2. Es posible que un conjunto de datos tenga más de una moda.

N

numerical data Values that are numbers such as counts, measurements, and ratings. Here are some examples.
- Number of children in families
- Pulse rates (number of heart beats per minute)
- Height
- Amount of time people spend reading in one day
- Amount of value placed on something, such as: on a scale of 1 to 5 with 1 as "low interest," how would you rate your interest in participating in the school's field day?

datos numéricos Valores que son números como, por ejemplo, cómputos, medidas y calificaciones. Aquí hay algunos ejemplos.
- Número de hijos e hijas en las familias
- Pulsaciones por minuto (número de latidos del corazón por minuto)
- Altura
- Cantidad de tiempo que las personas pasan leyendo en un día
- El valor que las personas le dan a algo, como por ejemplo: en una escala de 1 a 5, en la que 1 representa "poco interés", ¿cómo calificarías tu interés por participar en el día de campo de tu escuela?

O

outlier A value that lies far from the "center" of a distribution. Outlier is a relative term, but it indicates a data point that is much higher or much lower than the values that could be normally expected for the distribution.

valor extremo Valor que se sitúa lejos del "centro" de una distribución. El valor extremo es un término relativo, pero indica un dato que es mucho más alto o mucho más bajo que los valores que se podrían esperar normalmente de la distribución.

R

range The difference between the least value and the greatest value in a distribution. For example, in the distribution below, the range of the number of siblings is 8 people.

gama Diferencia entre el valor mínimo y máximo en una distribución. Por ejemplo, en la siguiente distribución, la gama del número de hermanos o hermanas es 8 personas.

Number of Siblings Students Have

```
                X
    X           X   X           X
    X   X   X   X   X   X
    X   X   X   X   X   X   X           X
    0   1   2   3   4   5   6   7   8
```

Number of Siblings

S

scale The size of the units on an axis of a graph or number line. For instance, each mark on the vertical axis might represent 10 units.

escala El tamaño de las unidades en un eje de una gráfica o recta numérica. Por ejemplo, cada marca en el eje vertical puede representar 10 unidades.

stem-and-leaf plot (stem plot) A quick way to picture the shape of a distribution while including the actual numerical values in the graph. For a number like 25, the stem 2 is written at the left of the vertical line, and the leaf, 5 is at the right.

diagrama de tallo y hojas Una manera rápida de representar la forma de una distribución y al mismo tiempo incluir los valores numéricos reales en la gráfica. Para un número como 25, el tallo 2 se escribe a la izquierda de la recta vertical, y la hoja 5, a la derecha de la recta.

Travel Time

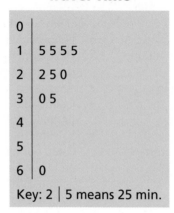

0	
1	5 5 5 5
2	2 5 0
3	0 5
4	
5	
6	0

Key: 2 | 5 means 25 min.

survey A method for collecting data that uses interviews. Surveys ask questions to find out information such as facts, opinions, or beliefs.

encuesta Un método para reunir datos que utiliza entrevistas. En las encuestas se hacen preguntas para averiguar información tal como hechos, opiniones o creencias.

T

table A tool for organizing information in rows and columns. Tables let you list categories or values and then tally the occurrences.

tabla Una herramienta para organizar información en filas y columnas. Las tablas permiten que se hagan listas de categorías o de valores y luego se computan los sucesos.

Favorite Colors

Color	Number of Students
Red	6
White	15
Blue	9

X

***x*-axis** The horizontal number line used to make a graph.

eje *x* Recta numérica horizontal que se usa para hacer una gráfica.

Y

***y*-axis** The vertical number line used to make a graph.

eje *y* Recta numérica vertical que se usa para hacer una gráfica.

Academic Vocabulary

The following terms are important to your understanding of the mathematics in this unit. Knowing and using these words will help you in thinking, reasoning, representing, communicating your ideas, and making connections across ideas. When these words make sense to you, the investigations and problems will make more sense as well.

A

analyze To study using a logical or mathematical system.

related terms: examine, evaluate, determine, observe, investigate

Sample: Analyze the following data to find the mean and the mode.

Getting to School

Student	Krista	Mike	Lupe	Kareem
Time (min)	10	15	20	10

The mean is $\frac{10 + 15 + 20 + 10}{4} = 13.75$.
The mode of this data is 10 because 10 is the value that occurs most often.

analizar Estudiar usando un sistema lógico o matemático.

términos relacionados: examinar, evaluar, determinar, observar, investigar

Ejemplo: Analiza los siguientes datos para hallar la media y la moda.

Tiempos a la escuela

Estudiante	Krista	Mike	Lupe	Kareem
Tiempo (minutos)	10	15	20	10

La media es $\frac{10 + 15 + 20 + 10}{4} = 13.75$.
La moda de estos datos es 10 porque 10 es el valor que ocurre con mayor frecuencia.

E

explain To give facts and details that make an idea easier to understand. Explaining can involve a written summary supported by a diagram, chart, table, or a combination of these.

related terms: analyze, clarify, describe, justify, tell

Sample: Explain why the mean may not be the best statistical measure of how many sit-ups students can do.

How many sit-ups?

```
0 | 9 9
1 | 0 1 2 2 5 5 6
2 |
3 |
4 | 1
Key 1 | 2 = 12
```

The mean is affected by the outlier 41, which is much greater than the rest of the data. The median or mode would be better measures of the data.

explicar Dar hechos y detalles que hacen que una idea sea más fácil de comprender. Explicar puede implicar un resumen escrito apoyado por hechos, un diagrama, una gráfica, una tabla o una combinación de éstos.

términos relacionados: analizar, aclarar, describir, justificar, decir

Ejemplo: Explica por qué la media puede no ser la mejor medida estadística de cuántas sentadillas pueden hacer los estudiantes.

¿Cuántas sentadillas?

```
0 | 9 9
1 | 0 1 2 2 5 5 6
2 |
3 |
4 | 1
Clave 1 | 2 = 12
```

La media se ve afectada por el valor extremo 41, que es mucho más grandes que el resto de los datos. La mediana o la moda serían mejores medidas de los datos.

predict To make an educated guess based on the analysis of real data.

related terms: estimate, guess, expect

Sample: **Dan knows that the mean life span of his type of tropical fish is 2 years. What other information could help Dan predict how long his fish will live?**

> If Dan also knew the median life span he would have more information to predict how long his fish will live. The mean could be skewed because of one or more outliers.

predecir Hacer una conjetura informada basada en el análisis de datos reales.

términos relacionados: estimar, conjeturar, esperar

Ejemplo: **Dan sabe que la duración de la vida media de su tipo de pez tropical es de 2 años. ¿Qué otra información podría ayudar a Dan a predecir cuánto vivirá su pez?**

> Si Dan también supiera la duración de la vida media, tendría más información para predecir cuánto vivirá su pez. La media podría estar sesgada debido a uno o más valores extremos.

represent To stand for or take the place of something else. Symbols, equations, charts, and tables are often used to represent particular situations.

related terms: symbolize, stand for

Sample: **Jerry surveyed his classmates about the number of pets they have. He recorded his data in a table. Represent the results of Jerry's survey in a bar graph.**

representar Significar o tomar el lugar de algo más. Con frecuencia se usan símbolos, ecuaciones, gráficas y tablas para representar situaciones particulares.

términos relacionados: simbolizar, significar

Ejemplo: **Jerry hizo una encuesta entre sus compañeros de clases sobre el número de mascotas que tienen. Anotó sus datos en una tabla. Representa los resultados de la encuesta de Jerry en una gráfica de barras.**

How Many Pets?

Number of Pets	Number of Students
0 pets	10
1 pet	11
2 or more pets	8

¿Cuántas mascotas?

Número de mascotas	Número de estudiantes
0 mascotas	10
1 mascota	11
2 ó más mascotas	8

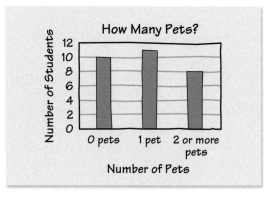

Index

Acknowledgments

Team Credits

The people who made up the **Connected Mathematics 2** team—representing editorial, editorial services, design services, and production services— are listed below. Bold type denotes core team members.

Leora Adler, Judith Buice, Kerry Cashman, Patrick Culleton, Sheila DeFazio, Richard Heater, **Barbara Hollingdale, Jayne Holman,** Karen Holtzman, **Etta Jacobs,** Christine Lee, Carolyn Lock, Catherine Maglio, **Dotti Marshall,** Rich McMahon, Eve Melnechuk, Kristin Mingrone, Terri Mitchell, **Marsha Novak,** Irene Rubin, Donna Russo, Robin Samper, Siri Schwartzman, **Nancy Smith,** Emily Soltanoff, **Mark Tricca,** Paula Vergith, Roberta Warshaw, Helen Young

Additional Credits

Diana Bonfilio, Mairead Reddin, Michael Torocsik, nSight, Inc.

Illustration

Michelle Barbera: 7, 20, 30, 59, 60

Technical Illustration

WestWords, Inc.

Cover Design

tom white.images

Photos

2 t, Chris Pinchbeck/IPN; **2 m,** Kwame Zikomo/SuperStock; **2 b,** Michael Newman/PhotoEdit; **3,** Jeff Greenberg/Peter Arnold, Inc.; **6,** Kwame Zikomo/SuperStock; **9,** Ariadne Van Zandbergen/Lonely Planet Images; **13,** Steve Vidler/SuperStock; **15 l,** Rick Gomez/Corbis; **15 r,** Myrleen Ferguson Cate/PhotoEdit; **18,** Ron Kimball/Ron Kimball Stock; **20,** Chris Pinchbeck/IPN; **23,** Ellen Senisi/The Image Works; **33,** Ray Stott/The Image Works; **35,** Kwame Zikomo/SuperStock; **36,** Richard Haynes; **38,** David Young-Wolff/PhotoEdit; **41,** Ellen Senisi/The Image Works; 43, Richard Haynes; **44,** Journal-Courier/Steve Warmowski/The Image Works; **47,** Jim Cummins/Getty Images, Inc.; **49,** Ron Stroud/Masterfile; **53,** Creatas/PictureQuest; **55,** Michael Newman/PhotoEdit; **57,** Bob Daemmrich Photography; **62,** Syracuse Newspapers/The Image Works; **65,** Joe McDonald/Corbis